POLITICAL TRIVIA
&
OTHER STUFF

SHERRIE LUEDER

To my grandchildren
Dakota, Breelynn, and every child
who was deprived of just having good
ole fashioned fun during the pandemic lockdowns.

"We crossed the threshold and felt as if we had just stepped out of our time machine walking into Belgium, Germany in 1941. One of the SS promptly demanded for a face mask to be placed on our faces. But sir we don't have one. Oh, you must pay and then you shall receive one. We only require it while you enter. You can remove it once you sit down. Is the seating 6 feet apart then?" No, he answered, we don't require that!

Jesse Lueder

Introduction

Fun and educational for all ages. Over 400 multiple choice questions and random facts presented as true or false. Hints (D) democrat and (R) republican as well as the year will help you with the answer.

Random questions in no specific order will present a challenge. Just when you're trying to figure out which state became the first in the U.S. to legalize the use of recreational marijuana, your brain is wondering which politician was asked to leave a Denver theater for disruptive behaviors. Please be kind and have fun!

1. February 4, 1789, the first presidential election was held. Who was unanimously chosen by electors to be the first president of the United States?
a) Thomas Jefferson
b) George Washington
c) Abraham Lincoln

2. A law degree is required to be a U.S. president.
a) true
b) false

3. (1776) What document declared the American colonies' independence from Great Britain?
a) The Constitution
b) The Emancipation Proclamation
c) The Declaration of Independence

4. (2020) The voters of which state passed the most liberal drug law in the country, decriminalizing possession for small amounts of hard drugs?
a) Washington
b) California
c) Oregon

5. The Civil War began primarily as a disagreement over the institution of slavery. It was fought between the northern and southern states between which years?
a) 1800-1820
b) 1861-1865
c) 1900-1910

Answers
1. b) George Washington
2. b) false
3. c) The Declaration of Independence
4. c) Oregon
5. b) 1861-1865

6. (2020) The first American case of what would become the Covid-19 coronavirus was confirmed. On March 13, President Trump declared a national emergency. In what country did the virus originate?
a) United States
b) Russia
c) China

7. Benjamin Franklin was a U.S. president.
a) true
b) false

8. (2018) While dining out with her family at a restaurant in Lexington Virginia, which White House press secretary was told to leave because she worked for President Trump
a) Jen Psaki
b) Sarah Sanders
c) Kayleigh McEnany

9. (2020) During the pandemic which California politician attended a birthday dinner party at the upscale French Laundry restaurant while seemingly ignoring face covering and social distancing guidelines?
a) Kamala Harris (D)
b) Gavin Newsome (D)
c) Kevin McCarthy (R)

Answers
6. b) China
7. b) false
8. b) Sarah Sanders
9. b) Gavin Newsome

10. U.S. presidents are required to live at the White House.
a) true
b) false

11. U.S. presidents and first families have taken part in a long-honored tradition of going by nicknames symbolic of their personalities or legacies. Which name did former President Trump choose as his nickname?
a) Maga
b) Mogul
c) Miracle

12. (2021) What federal holiday did President Joe Biden sign into law to commemorate the ending of slavery?
a) Martin Luther King Jr. Day
b) Juneteenth
c) Labor Day

13. (2023) While attending a performance of the "Beetlejuice" musical at the Buell Theatre in Denver, Colorado, which politician and guest were asked to leave due to their disruptive behavior following other attendee's complaints that they were vaping and singing?
a) Lauren Boebert (R)
b) Jason Crow (D)
c) Diane DeGette (D)

Answers
10. b) false
11. b) Mogul
12. b) Juneteenth
13. a) Lauren Boebert (R)

14. (1787) What became the first state after ratifying the constitution?
a) Florida
b) Colorado
c) Delaware

15. (2016) During an LGBT campaign fundraising event in New York City, while giving a speech, who said the following? "You know, to just be grossly generalistic, you could put half of Trump's supporters into what I call the basket of deplorables. They're racist, sexist, homophobic, xenophobic, Islamophobic you name it. And unfortunately, there are people like that."
a) Bernie Sanders (D)
b) Jeb Bush (D)
c) Hillary Clinton (D)

16. The secret service refers to the president, First Lady and other officials by a code name. What was President Obama's code name?
a) Mogul
b) Celtic
c) Renegade

17. (2014) Which state became the first in the U.S. to legalize the use of recreational marijuana?
a) Washington
b) Colorado
c) California

Answers
14. c) Delaware
15. c) Hillary Clinton (D)
16. c) Renegade
17. b) Colorado

18. (2019) Attorney General William Barr was scheduled to testify before the House Judiciary Committee but was unable to attend. Who took the opportunity to highlight Barr's absence by bringing a bucket of KFC chicken, eating it, and then placing it in front of Barr's empty seat?
a) Steve Cohen (D)
b) Jerry Nadler (D)
c) Marjorie Taylor Greene (R)

19. (2023) Hundreds of queer activists attended an LGBTQ+ Pride event hosted by the Biden administration. Three transgender attendees were banned from attending future events at the White House for doing which of the following?
a) shouting profanities at President Biden
b) carrying Trump 2024 flags
c) baring their chests

20. (2016) Which politician promoted the falsehood that Barack Obama was not born in the United States? And continued saying it for five more years until finally back-peddling admitting he was wrong.
a) Mitt Romney (R)
b) John McCain (R)
c) Donald Trump (R)

21. (1861) Who was elected as the 16th president of the United States and served until his assassination in 1865?
a) Andrew Johson (D)
b) Abraham Lincoln (R)
c) James Buchanan (D)

Answer
18. a) Steve Cohen (D)
19. c) baring their chests
20. c) Donald Trump (R)
21. b) Abraham Lincoln (R)

22. (1986) When asked to identify her race, which politician falsely wrote on her Texas bar registration card "American Indian?" Later President Donald Trump would ridicule her for claiming to be of "North American Heritage" and referred to her as "Pocahontas."
a) Elizabeth Warren (D)
b) Tammy Baldwin (D)
c) Tammy Duckworth (D)

23. (1981) Which president survived an attempted assassination after being shot with a revolver?
a) George H. W. Bush
b) Ronald Regan
c) Jimmy Carter

24. (2024) Non-binary Sam Brinton was charged a third time for stealing women's luggage and was freed on bond after spending over two weeks in jail. Which position did Brinton hold in the Biden administration?
a) Secretary of Transportation
b) Secretary of Energy
c) Deputy Secretary of the office of Nuclear Energy

25. It is well known that President Joe Biden loves this sweet treat.
a) jellybeans
b) licorice
c) ice cream

Answers
22. a) Elizabeth Warren
23. b) Ronald Regan
24. c) Deputy Secretary of the office of Nuclear Energy
25. c) ice cream

26. (2024) Who is the director of the Federal Bureau of Investigation?
a) Christopher Wray
b) Andrew McCabe
c) James Comey

27. Christmas is a federal holiday.
a) true
b) false

28. (1961) John F. Kennedy took the oath of office to become the nation's 35th president. His inaugural address inspired many with which quote?
a) "Believe you can and you're half-way there."
b) "Ask not what your country can do for you – ask what you can do for your country."
c) "No person was ever honored for what he received. Honor has been the reward for what he gave."

29. (2024) Records released from the Secret Service reveal Joe Biden's dog was involved in at least 25 biting incidents in less than a year. The German shepherd has since been banished from the White House. What was the dog's name?
a) Freedom
b) Lancer
c) Commander

Answers
26. a) Christopher Wray
27. a) true
28. b) "Ask not what your country can do for you – ask what you can do for your country."
29. c) Commander

30. (1854) The Republican Party (GOP) was founded by anti-slavery expansion activists and modernizers. Where was it founded?
a) Spirit Lake, Iowa
b) Rippon, Wisconsin
c) Sycamore, Illinois

31. (2023) Which representative from New York knowingly pulled a fire alarm, causing an evacuation, while the House was voting to keep the government funded?
a) Jamaal Bowman (D)
b) Alexandria Ocasio-Cortez (D)
c) Elise Stefanik (R)

32. As of 2024 who is the first president in history to face a criminal trial?
a) Richard Nixon
b) Bill Clinton
c) Donald Trump

33. (2016) Which Ohio Senator wrote the bestselling memoir, Hillbilly Elegy, which was later adapted into a film?
a) J. D. Vance (R)
b) Sherrod Brown (D)
c) Jim Jordan (R)

Answers
30. b) Rippon, Wisconsin
31. a) Jamaal Bowman (D)
32. c) Donald Trump
33. a) J.D. Vance

34. (2020) Which democratic squad member was under investigation for allegedly marrying her brother to ease his immigration into the United States?
a) Rashida Tlaib
b) Cori Bush
c) Ilhan Omar

35. (2013) Bridgegate was a political scandal that involved a staff member and governor appointees colluding to cause New Jersey traffic jams by closing lanes at the main toll plaza. Who was the governor that appointed those involved?
a) Chris Christie (R)
b) Phil Murphy (D)
c) Andy Kim (D

36. As of 2024 how many dogs have lived in the white house?
a) 31
b) 36
c) 48

37. Which president dodged the draft after receiving five student draft deferments from the Vietnam War and a medical exemption claiming he had asthma as a teenager?
a) Bill Clinton (D
b) Joe Biden (D)
c) Donald Trump (D)

Answers
34. c) Ilhan Omar
35. a) Chris Christie (R)
36. a) 31
37. b) Joe Biden (D)

38. Before becoming vice president, Kamala Harris served as Attorney General for which state?
a) New York
b) Arizona
c) California

39. Every U.S. president is buried at Arlington National Cemetery when they die.
a) true
b) false

40. After decades of endorsing a democrat, the Teamsters decided not to make an endorsement for the 2024 presidential election.
a) true
b) false

41. (2024) As of June 10, how many candidates had registered for the 2024 presidential election?
a) 3
b) 25
c) 1,000+

42. (1841) Which president died after serving only 31 days as president?
a) William Harrison
b) John Tyler
c) Andrew Jackson

Answers
38. c) California
39. b) false
40. a) true
41. c) 1000+
42. a) William Harrison

43. (2017) Twenty-four Republican congressmen had gathered to practice for the Congressional Baseball Game when a left-wing activist shot six people. Which congressman was shot?
a) John Rhodes
b) Steve Scalise
c) Tom Emmer

44. (2024) The Attorney General leads the Justice Department's 115,000 employees, who work across the United States and in more than 50 countries worldwide. Who is he?
a) William Barr
b) Jeff Sessions
c) Merrick Garland

45. (2020) As President Trump finished delivering the State of the Union Address, who stood up and tore it in half?
a) Paul Ryan
b) Nancy Pelosi
c) Kevin McCarthy

46. January 6, 2021- A mob of rioters stormed the capitol for what reason?
a) to support the president elect
b) to support abortion
c) to stop the election certification

Answers
43. b) Steve Scalise
44. c) Merrick Garland
45. b) Nancy Pelosi
46. c) to stop the election certification

47. How many United States Supreme Court justices are there?
a) 6
b) 9
c) 12

48. (1868-2021) Three presidents have been impeached although none have been removed from office. Which president was impeached twice?
a) Andrew Johnson
b) Bill Clinton
c) Donald Trump

49. How many United States presidents are buried at Arlington National Cemetery?
a) 30
b) 0
c) 2

50. (2024) The House of Representatives voted to approve more money in aid to Ukraine to support the war, as Democrats waved the country's flag and chanted "Ukraine, Ukraine, Ukraine." As of May 9, the United States has given Ukraine a total of how many dollars?
a) 175 billion
b) 60 billion
c) 500 million

Answers
47. b) 9
48. c) Donald Trump
49. c) 2
50. a) 175 billion

51. Every two years the members of the U.S. House of Representatives vote for a speaker on the first day of each new congress. Who was the longest serving Democratic Speaker of the House of Representatives as of the year 2024?
a) Sam Rayburn
b) Nancy Pelosi
c) Thomas Phillip "Tip" O' Neil Jr.

52. (2023) Which Democratic politician serving the Rhode Island Senate was charged with vandalism/malicious injury to property and obstruction of a police officer after keying a vehicle that had a "Biden sucks" bumper sticker on it?
a) Joshua Miller
b) Matthew LaMountain
c) Frank Lombard

53. (1996) Which state became the first to legalize the use of medical marijuana?
a) New York
b) Hawaii
c) California

54. As of April 2024, recreational marijuana was legalized in how many states?
a) 24 states
b) 5 states
c) 50 states

Answers
51. a) Sam Rayburn
52. a) Joshua Miller
53. c) California
54. a) 24 states

55. (2020) The supreme court was in session hearing arguments on a major abortion case. Referring to the judges, which senator stepped onto the courthouse steps and loudly announced to the crowd? "I want to tell you Gorsuch. I want to tell you Kavanaugh. You have released the whirlwind, and you will pay the price. You won't know what hit you if you go forward with these decisions."
a) Chuck Schumer (D)
b) Ted Cruz (R)
c) Kyrsten Sinema (D)

56. (2020) Amid the coronavirus pandemic, rules were in place that kept businesses shuttered and forced people to wear a face covering. Despite the rules which politician was captured on security video visiting a San Francisco hair salon and moving around without a face covering?
a) Adam Schiff (D)
b) Nancy Pelosi (D)
c) Maxine Waters (D)

57. (1955) Which state was given the exclusive rights to use the "Land of Lincoln" insignia as their slogan?
a) Indiana
b) Ohio
c) Illinois

Answers
55. a) Chuck Schumer (D)
56. b) Nancy Pelosi
57. c) Illinois

58. (2020) In the aftermath of the death of George Floyd there were several riots and protests in Minneapolis/St. Paul that resulted in extensive damage and looting as well as destroying a police station. Several rioters were arrested. Which politician took to social media asking, "If you're able to, chip in now to the Minnesota Freedom Fund to help post bail for those protesting on the ground in Minnesota?"
a) Ilhan Omar (D)
b) Sheila Jackson (D)
c) Kamala Harris (D)

59. (2016) Democrat presidential candidate Hillary Clinton announced on Twitter who she had chosen as her vice-presidential running mate. Which of the following did she choose?
a) Tim Kaine
b) Corey Booker
c) Elizabeth Warren

60. Who was the longest serving Republican Speaker of the House of Representatives as of the year 2024?
a) Newt Gingrich
b) John Boehner
c) John Hastert

61. What happens to a presidential car when it is taken out of commission?
a) a president may buy it
b) it is destroyed by the Secret Service
c) sold in a government auction

Answers
58. c) Kamala Harris
59. a) Tim Kaine
60. c) John Hastert
61. b) it is destroyed by the Secret Service

62. By the 1860's an estimated one third of the United States currency in circulation was counterfeit. On April 14, 1865, which president established the United States Secret Service to prevent the counterfeiting of money?
a) Andrew Johnson (D)
b) Abraham Lincoln (R)
c) Ulysses S. Grant (R)

63. From 1789 to 2024 how many presidents have held the office of the presidency?
a) 40
b) 46
c) 50

64. (1918) The first $10,000 bill was printed. The Fed and Treasury discontinued the bill in 1969. The following three men's faces appear on currency. Which face is on the $10,000 note?
a) James Madison
b) Salmon P. Chase
c) Benjamin Franklin

65. President John Quincy Adams had a pet alligator that lived in the East Room bathtub.
a) true
b) false

66. If you see someone flying their flag upside down, it could mean that they need your help.
a) true
b) false

Answers
62. b) Abraham Lincoln
63. b) 46
64. b) Salmon P. Chase
65. a) true
66. a) true

67. Franklin D. Roosevelt was the first president to travel on official business by airplane.
a) true
b) false

68. (1988) Which United States President suffered 2 life threatening brain aneurysms?
a) Ronald Reagan
b) Joe Biden
c) Richard Nixon

69. (2015) D.C. license plates GG-300 were auctioned and sold for $100,000. Which presidential car were the plates removed from?
a) President Barack Obama
b) President Donald Trump
c) John F. Kennedy

70. The presidential limousine is equipped with a refrigerator containing the United States Presidents blood type.
a) true
b) false

71. (2024) Who was the third-party candidate in the 2024 presidential election?
a) Nikki Haley
b) Gavin Newsom
c) Robert F. Kennedy Jr.

Answers
67. a) true
68. b) Joe Biden
69. c) John F. Kennedy
70. a) true
71. c) Robert F. Kennedy Jr.

72. Which is the largest of the 50 United States?
a) Texas
b) Alaska
c) California

73. (2020) In response to the coronavirus pandemic governors from 43 states issued orders directing nonessential businesses to close and residents to stay home. How many republican governors kept their states open?
a) 7
b) 5
c) 9

74. (2016) The "Lock her up chant" originated at a Republican National Convention calling for which of the following politicians to be put in prison for using a private email server while serving as Secretary of State?
a) Hillary Clinton
b) Condoleezza Rice
c) John Kerry

75. (2020) At a New Hampshire campaign event a presidential candidate asked a college student if she had ever been to a caucus. When she replied "yes," the candidate said, "No, you haven't, you're a lying dog-faced pony soldier." Who said it?
a) Kanye West
b) Donald Trump
c) Joe Biden

Answers
72. b) Alaska
73. c) 7
74. a) Hillary Clinton
75. c) Joe Biden

76. John F. Kennedy's presidential car, a 1961 Lincoln Continental, was originally a stock car.
a) true
b) false

77. (2024) President Donald Trump held a rally in the Bronx. This didn't sit well with a certain New York politician who said in an interview. "I'll tell you what won't make a difference at all, and that's for Donald Trump to be the ringleader and invite all his clowns to a place like the Bronx." Which politician referred to Trump supporters as "Clowns?"
a) Letitia James-Attorney General
b) Kathy Hochul-Governor
c) Eric Adams-Mayor

78. (2024) In a book written by South Dakota Governor Kristi Noem she described how she hated the family dog and realized she had to put her down. The day she took her dog to a gravel pit to shoot her she also shot something else. What was it?
a) her horse
b) her goat
c) her truck

79. Over the last few years, the terminology of someone entering the U.S. illegally went through several changes with the help of the Democrats and the mainstream media. The correct term to use as of 2024 is what?
a) newcomers
b) helpers
c) visitors

Answers
76. a) true
77. b) Kathy Hochul-Governor
78. b) her goat
79. a) newcomers

80. (2018) In referring to Trump administration officials, which California politician rallied her followers by shrilling "If you see anybody from that cabinet in a restaurant, in a department store, at a gasoline station, you get out and you create a crowd and you push back on them, and you tell them they're not welcome anymore, anywhere?"
a) Tina Smith
b) Maxine Waters
c) Debbie Stabenow

81. The Bill of Rights is the first 10 Amendments to the Constitution. It spells out Americans' rights in relation to their government. What Amendment protects the right to keep and bear arms?
a) Second Amendment
b) Eighth Amendment
c) Seventh Amendment

82. Which president, while holding office, deported the most illegal immigrants? So much so that he was nicknamed the "Deporter in Chief" by critics in the immigrant-rights community.
a) George W. Bush (R)
b) Donald Trump (R)
c) Barack Obama (D)

83. United States presidents must pay taxes on their yearly salary?
a) true
b) false

Answers
80. b) Maxine Waters
81. a) Second Amendment
82. c) Barack Obama (D)
83. a) true

84. (1983) During a family vacation a future politician drove 12 hours with his dog strapped to the top of his car in what he described as an "air-tight kennel" with windshield wipers that the dog enjoyed. The incident drew negative media attention in 2018 when the individual ran for president. Who was he?
a) John McCain
b) Rudy Giuliana
c) Mitt Romney

85. (2024) The federal minimum wage in the United States is $7.25. Which state set the minimum wage at $20.00 for fast food workers as of May 2024?
a) New York
b) California
c) Florida

86.The Apprentice is a reality television series that ran from 2008 to 2015. Which president played a starring role in the series?
a) Donald Trump
b) Ronald Regan
c) Bill Clinton

87. (1990) Which president did not like broccoli and would not allow it to be served in the White House or on Air Force One.
a) George H. W. Bush
b) Woodrow Wilson
c) Joe Biden

Answers
84. c) Mitt Romney
85. b) California
86. c) Donald trump
87. a) George H. W. Bush

88. (2020) The Capitol Hill Autonomous Zone was an unlawful occupation protest set up by people protesting the killing of George Floyd. The zone was established on June 8th and was cleared of occupants by police on July 1. The city's mayor, Jenny Durkan, suggested it could simply be a "summer of love." Where was the CHAZ zone also known as the CHOP zone?
a) Capitol Hill neighborhood of Seattle, Washington
b) Capitol Hill neighborhood of Washington D.C.
c) Capitol Hill neighborhood of Minneapolis, Minnesota

89. (2018) Which candidate refused to concede the gubernatorial election to Republican Brian Kemp after losing by 60,000 votes?
a) John Cox (R) California
b) Stacey Abrams (D) Georgia
c) Scott Walker (R) Wisconsin

90. The Democratic Party was founded in 1828. It was formed as a vehicle to elect Andrew Jackson of Tennessee for president of the United States. Where was the party formed?
a) Washington D.C.
b) Philadelphia, Pennsylvania
c) Providence, Rhode Island

91. The president and vice president can reside in the same state.
a) true
b) false

Answers
88. a) Capitol Hill neighborhood of Seattle, Washington
89. b) Stacey Abrams (D) Georgia
90. a) Washington D.C.
91. b) false

92. (2022) At the lengthy confirmation hearing for Supreme Court nominee Judge Ketanji Brown Jackson she was asked by Senator Marsha Blackburn to define which of the following terms? And her response was. "I can't. Not in this context. I'm not a biologist."
a) woman
b) transgender
c) gender

93. What document is known as the supreme law of the land?
a) The Constitution
b) The Declaration of Independence
c) The Bill of Rights

94. (2021) "I pledge to be a president who seeks not to divide, but to unify, who doesn't see red states and blue states, only sees the United States." Which president said this in their victory speech?
a) Joe Biden
b) Donald Trump
c) Barack Obama

95. (2024) Nearly forty years ago a tree fell on Governor Greg Abbott while he was out jogging and left him paralyzed from the waist down. What state does he currently represent?
a) Louisiana
b) Ohio
c) Texas

Answers
92. a) woman
93. a) The Constitution
94. a) Joe Biden
95. c) Texas

96. (2024) Documents show the Secret Service determined that presidential candidate Robert F. Kennedy was the subject of threats from "known subjects" but for the fifth time has been denied Secret Service protection. Who makes the final decision to appoint security detail to a candidate?
a) the sitting president
b) the vice president
c) the Secretary of Homeland Security

97. (2022) When FBI agents raided Mar-a-Lago in search of classified documents Melania Trump felt violated and bought new things because she felt her belongings had been "contaminated." What did the former First Lady buy?
a) underwear
b) car
c) purse

98. Who is the only United States President who was elected as an independent?
a) George Washington
b) John Tyler
c) Millard Fillmore

99. Who is the only person who served as president of the United States without being elected?
a) Richard Nixon
b) Gerald Ford
c) Spiro Agnew

Answers
96. c) the Secretary of Homeland Security
97. a) underwear
98. a) George Washington
99. b) Gerald Ford

100. (1953) Camp David received its present name from which president?
a) Dwight D. Eisenhower
b) Harry S. Truman
c) John F. Kennedy

101. (2019) During the second democratic debate when candidates were asked if they would decriminalize illegal immigration all but one of the 10 candidates raised their hand. Who was it?
a) Kamala Harris-California Senator
b) Michael Bennet-Colorado Senator
c) Joe Biden-Delaware Senator

102. What is the national bird of the United States?
a) robin
b) eagle
c) raven

103. What is the national flower of the United States?
a) rose
b) daisy
c) sunflower

104. What is the national tree of the United States?
a) maple
b) oak
c) willow

Answers
100. a) Dwight D. Eisenhower
101. b) Michael Bennet-Colorado Senator
102. b) eagle
103. a) rose
104. b) oak

105. Joe Biden served as Vice President to which president?
a) Barack Obama
b) Bill Clinton
c) Jimmy Carter

106. The sculptures of 4 heads of United States presidents are carved into Mount Rushmore. Which state is the sculpture in?
a) South Dakota
b) Montana
c) Washington

107. Which politician served as the second President of the United States after serving as the first vice president to George Washington?
a) John Adams
b) John Quincy Adams
c) Thomas Jefferson

108. (2020) During an interview with radio host, Charlamagne Tha God, which of the presidential candidates said, "if you have a problem figuring out who to vote for then you ain't black?"
a) Donald Trump
b) Joe Biden
c) Barack Obama

Answers
105. a) Barack Obama
106. a) South Dakota
107. a) John Adams
108. b) Joe Biden

109. What is the First Lady Jill Biden's code name?
a) Capri
b) April
c) September

110. The White House was constructed between 1792 and 1800. Who was the first president to reside there?
a) John Adams
b) George Washington
c) James Monroe

111. (1909) The Congressional Baseball Game began with members of congress, Republicans and Democrats, each forming separate teams. In 1979 who was the first congressman ever to hit a home run over the fence?
a) Ron Paul (R)
b) Jerry Nadler (D)
c) George Aiken (R)

112. The ghost of President William Harrison is said to have lingered in the White House several years after his death, but who is the most famous ghost to haunt the White House?
a) John F. Kennedy
b) Richard Nixon
c) Abraham Lincoln

Answers
109. a) Capri
110. a) John Adams
111. a) Ron Paul (R)
112. c) Abraham Lincoln

113. (2024) A group of climate change protesters disrupted the annual Charity Congressional Baseball Game, but it didn't stop this congressman from hitting an out-of-the-park homer. The first in over 40 years. Who was he?
a) Greg Steube (R)
b) Corey Booker (D)
c) Ron DeSantis (R)

114. (2022) Truth Social is a social media platform launched by Donald Trump after he was banned from other social media sites. Which politician quit his job to join the company?
a) Eric Swalwell (D)
b) David Nunes (R)
c) Tom McClintock (R)

115. January 6, 2021, QAnon Shaman-Jacob Chansley was sentenced to 41 months for obstructing an official proceeding at the Capitol. He was released a year early after video footage of the rioters showed he was wrongly sentenced. What does the footage show?
a) he never entered the Capitol
b) sitting at Nancy Pelosi's desk
c) police giving him a tour of the Capitol

Answers
113. a) Greg Steube (R)
114. b) David Nunes (R)
115. c) police giving him a tour of the Capitol

116. (1998) Which president ended his televised remarks with the later infamous statement? "I did not have sexual relations with that woman, Ms. Lewinsky."
a) Bill Clinton
b) George W. Bush
c) Donald Trump

117. Since February 2021, unaccompanied child encounters at the border have consistently exceeded 8,500 per month. What happens to these children?
a) they are housed at the border until someone claims them
b) they are deported
c) they are transferred to the Office of Refugee Resettlement

118. (2023) Governor Pritzker was the first to sign into law a bill ending the use of cash bail in which state?
a) California
b) Illinois
c) Florida

119. (2019) In an historic moment, who was the first United States sitting president to enter North Korea?
a) Jimmy Carter
b) Bill Clinton
c) Donald Trump

120. Only United States presidents are pictured on paper currency.
a) true
b) false

Answers
116. a) Bill Clinton
117. c) they are transferred to the Office of Refugee Resettlement
118. b) Illinois
119. c) Donald Trump
120. b) false

121. (2019) Which politician nicknamed North Korean leader Kim Jong Un "Little Rocket Man?"
a) Hillary Clinton
b) Donald Trump
c) Joe Biden

122. Pursuant to the Gun Control Act, it is unlawful for any person who is an illegal immigrant in the United States to possess any firearm or ammunition. What circumstances make it legal for them to possess a firearm?
a) when using it for protection
b) when employed as a law enforcement officer
c) when traveling back to their country of origin

123. (2024) Democratic Governor Jay Inslee signed legislation that allows undocumented immigrants, who first arrived in the United States as children, to apply for positions at the Police Department. What state is this?
a) Illinois
b) Wisconsin
c) Washington

124. (2017) Which singer dubbed the "Queen of Pop" told a crowd at the Women's March on Washington that she had, "thought an awful lot about blowing up the White House?"
a) Cyndi Lauper
b) Madonna
c) Gwen Stefani

Answers
121. b) Donald Trump
122. b) when employed as a law enforcement officer
123. c) Washington
124. b) Madonna

125. (2024) Pastor Lorenzo Sewell of 180 Church in Detroit expressed gratitude that a president visited the "hood." He also criticized presidents who never visited. Which president visited the "hood?"
a) Donald Trump
b) Barack Obama
c) Joe Biden

126. (1870) New Years Day, Independence Day, Thanksgiving, and Christmas were the first federal holidays signed into law by which president?
a) George Washington
b) Abraham Lincoln
c) Ulysses S. Grant

127. The youngest man to serve as president of the United States was 43 years old when he took office. Who was he?
a) Bill Clinton
b) John F. Kennedy
c) Jimmy Carter

128. (2024) How many men are currently serving on the United States Supreme Court?
a) 3
b) 7
c) 5

Answers
125. a) Donald Trump
126. c) Ulysses S. Grant
127. b) John F. Kennedy
128. c) 5

129. The oldest man to serve as president of the United States was 78 years old when he took office. Who is he?
a) Ronald Reagan
b) William Henry Harrison
c) Joe Biden

130. The lowest governors' salary is $70,000. Which state is it?
a) Texas
b) California
c) Maine

131. (1970) Richard Nixon met with this rock star at the White House after he requested a visit in a six-page letter to the president. In the letter he wrote. "I would love to meet you just to say hello if you're not too busy." Who was he?
a) Freddie Mercury
b) Elvis Presley
c) Elton John

132. (2020) While campaigning for president, which candidate promised a tax credit of up to $15,000 for first time home buyers if elected, but never delivered?
a) Howie Hawkins (G)
b) Joe Biden (D)
c) Donald Trump) (R)

Answers
129. c) Joe Biden
130. c) Maine
131. b) Elvis Presley
132. b) Joe Biden (D)

133. Hi-Catoctin was built as a retreat for federal government agents and their families. In 1942, President Franklin D. Roosevelt converted it to a presidential retreat and renamed it what?
a) Shangri-la
b) Rehoboth Beach
c) Martha's Vineyard

134. Camp David sits in Catoctin Mountain Park and the map does not indicate the location due to privacy and security concerns. What state is Camp David located in?
a) Maryland
b) Virginia
c) Florida

135. (2024) The left is pushing a campaign strategy that if Donald Trump wins the election, he will destroy American democracy. What is democracy?
a) a system where one government rules the people
b) a system of government that is directly exercised by the people or through their elected representatives
c) a system where one person makes all the decisions

136. Although 12 amendments to the Constitution were originally proposed, 10 were ratified to become the Bill of Rights in 1791. As of 2024 how many amendments are in the constitution?
a) 27
b) 33
c) 20

Answers
133. a) Shangri-La
134. a) Maryland
135. b b) a system of government that is directly exercised by the people or through their elected representatives
136. a) 27

137. What date did the Continental Congress adopt the Declaration of Independence?
a) July 4, 1776
b) June 14, 1776
c) July 4, 1876

138. President Theodore Roosevelt showed his love for animals when on a hunting trip he refused to shoot one. Subsequently a toy was named in his honor. What was it?
a) bunny rabbit
b) teddy bear
c) reindeer

139. (2017) A fake news story circulated several times falsely claiming that former President Barack Obama would replace George Washington on the $1 bill. Why was the story deemed fake?
a) Barack Obama did not want his portrait on any currency
b) Congress issued an act stating no living person can appear on U.S. currency
c) Obama wanted his portrait on the penny

140. (1959) Under the Eisenhower Administration what became our fiftieth state?
a) Texas
b) Florida
c) Hawaii

Answers
137. a) July 4, 1776
138. c) teddy bear
139. b) Congress issued an act stating no living person can appear on U.S. currency
140. c) Hawaii

141. On October 1, 1924, in Plains, Georgia which was the first president to be born in a hospital?
a) Gerald Ford
b) Jimmy Carter
c) George H.W. Bush

142. On June 21, 1788, the Constitution became the official framework of the government of the United States when which of the following became the ninth state to ratify it?
a) New Hampshire
b) Alaska
c) Ohio

143. (1787) The second state to become a state was also where the Declaration of Independence was signed and where the Constitution was created. Which state was it?
a) Washington
b) Pennsylvania
C) Virginia

144. (2023) The Secret Service found an unknown substance inside a vestibule leading to the lobby area of the West Executive Avenue entrance to the White House. What was the substance?
a) marijuana
b) it was undetermined
c) cocaine

Answers
141. b) Jimmy Carter
142. a) New Hampshire
143. b) Pennsylvania
144. c) cocaine

145. (2023) What was the outcome of the Secret Service investigation into the discovery of cocaine found at the White House?
a) the perpetrator was discovered on the video footage and charged
b) the investigation was closed due to lack of physical evidence
c) the perpetrator was found and cleared of any wrongdoing

146. During the 2024 presidential debate President Biden accused Donald Trump of putting babies in cages at the southern border. Who oversaw the construction of the "cages" to begin with?
a) Trump/Pence administration
b) Obama/Biden administration
c) they had been constructed years before

147. Former president Lyndon B. Johnson named his pet beagles Him and Her. During Johnson's stay at the White House Him met an unfortunate death. How did he die?
a) he got stuck in an elevator door
b) he was poisoned
c) he was run over by the presidential limousine

148. Former president Ronald Reagan's dog Rex, sensing something unnatural, frantically barked and refused to enter which room in the White House?
a) kitchen
b) Lincoln Bedroom
c) Oval Office

Answers
145. b) the investigation was closed due to lack of physical evidence
146. b) Obama/Biden administration
147. c) he was run over by the presidential limousine
148. b) Lincoln bedroom

149. Former president William Taft admonished one of his military aides for writing about the following and threatened to fire any staffers who repeated the story.
a) his dog biting him
b) a ghostly apparition in the White House
c) him accidentally shooting his foot

150. How many presidential limousines are used in the United States?
a) at least 10
b) 50
c) 25

151. During their stay at the White House what unexplained sound did George W. Bush's twin daughters hear coming from the fireplace?
a) screaming
b) piano music
c) whispering

152. During the Obama's stay at the White House, other than hearing strange noises in the hallway at night, some family members witnessed other unexplained phenomena. What was it?
a) feeling of tapping on their shoulder
b) feeling of something tugging on their hair
c) feeling of something gnawing or chewing on their feet

Answers
149. b) a ghostly apparition in the White House
150. a) at least 10
151. b) piano music
152. c) feeling of something gnawing or chewing on their feet

153. (1908) The Bureau of Investigation (BOI) was founded by Teddy Roosevelt to do what?
a) investigate corruption in the government.
b) investigate common criminals
c) investigate organized crime

154. Presidential limousines are transported by military cargo ships when the president travels abroad.
a) true
b) false

155. William Howard Taft is one of 2 presidents buried at Arlington National cemetery. Who became the second president buried there in 1963?
a) George H. W. Bush
b) John F. Kennedy
c) James K. Polk

156. (2003) Twenty-two agencies unified to form the Department of Homeland Security with the common mission of safeguarding the American people. Which president established (DHS)?
a) Bill Clinton (D)
b) George W. Bush (R)
c) George H. W. Bush (R)

Answers
153. a) investigate corruption in the government
154. a) true
155. b) John F. Kennedy
156. b) George W. Bush (R)

157. (1939) President Teddy Roosevelt received the first presidential car, a Lincoln convertible called the "Sunshine Special," which was built to Secret Service specifications. Why was it named the Sunshine Special?
a) it was painted yellow
b) the top was frequently open
c) he received it on a sunny day

158. July 11, 2024, the house passed the SAVE Act bill requiring documentary proof of United States citizenship to vote. The vote was 221 to 198. Most Democrats voted against it.
a) true
b) false

159. (2021) More than 8,000 United States service members were discharged from the military for refusing to be vaccinated against Covid-19. Who mandated the vaccine for the military?
a) Defense Secretary Lloyd Austin
b) President Joe Biden
c) Anthony Fauci

160. (2017) A Bismarck, North Dakota man hatched a plan to kill President Trump as he traveled through Mandan, North Dakota in his motorcade. His plan was to get to the President after first flipping his limo using which piece of machinery?
a) dump truck
b) forklift
c) military tank

Answers
157. b) the top was frequently open
158. a) true
159. a) Defense Secretary Lloyd Austin
160. b) forklift

161. (2024) Which State Supreme Court reversed its own 2022 decision that rejected the use of drop boxes, deciding in a 4-3 vote that a ballot does not have to be returned in person?
a) Florida
b) Wisconsin
c) Iowa

162. (2024) Where was the first presidential debate held between President Joe Biden and former President Donald Trump?
a) Cleveland, Ohio
b) Atlanta, Georgia
c) Chicago, Illinois

163. President Grover Cleveland oversaw the dedication of the Statue of Liberty, which was gifted to the United States on July 4, 1884, by the people of which country?
a) Great Britain
b) Canada
c) France

164. Which Representative for the state of New York was a bartender before entering into politics?
a) Jeffries Hakeem
b) Alexandria Ocasio Cortez
c) Elsie Stefanik

Answers
161. b) Wisconsin
162. c) Atlanta, Georgia
163. c) France
164. b) Alexandria Ocasio Cortez

165. (2024) To help deter immigrants from crossing the border illegally the Texas National Guard began to install razor wire. President Biden ordered federal officials to cut the razor wire. Is It true or false that Texas governor Abbott ordered it to be put back up again?
a) true
b) false

166. (2024) "I have one job, and that's to beat Donald Trump. I'm absolutely certain I'm the best person to be able to do that. So, we're done talking about the debate, it's time to put Trump in a bullseye." Who said it?
a) Kamala Harris
b) Joe Biden
c) Hillary Clinton

167. (2024) Presidential candidate Donald Trump was shot while speaking at a rally in which city?
a) Butler, Pennsylvania
b) Minneapolis, Minnesota
c) Des Moines, Iowa

168. (2024) Biden opposed the Safeguard American Voter Eligibility (SAVE) Act, which would require people to provide proof of citizenship to register to vote.
a) true
b) false

Answers
165. a) true
166. b) Joe Biden
167. a) Butler, Pennsylvania
168. a) true

169. As of July 2024, over a dozen municipalities in the U.S. allow undocumented immigrants to vote in local elections.
a) true
b) false

170. (2024) Elon Musk pledged 45 million a month to a new PAC supporting which candidate running for president?
a) Vivek Ramaswamy
b) Donald Trump
c) Joe Biden

171. (2024) At the RNC convention when delivering a speech, which Republican speaker said the following? "Americans cannot afford another 'Weekend at Bernie's' presidency."
a) Ron DeSantis
b) Donald Trump
c) Ron Johnson

172. Former President Thomas Jefferson's portrait is on the obverse side of the nickel. The building on the reverse is "Monticello." What is it?
a) a law school
b) Jefferson's home
c) a library

Answers
169. a) true
170. b) Donald Trump
171. a) Ron DeSantis
172. b) Jefferson's home

173. (2024) Democrats promote the falsehood that former President Trump called the Veterans who lost their lives "suckers and losers." As written in a news article, the source of the information came from who?
a) Kellyanne Conway
b) Mitch McConnell
c) Trump's senior staffers

174. (2024) Presidential candidate Robert F. Kennedy Jr. was finally granted secret service protection shortly after the attempted assassination of Donald Trump.
a) true
b) false

175. (2024) The Republican National Convention was held during the week of July 15 in which city?
a) Chicago, Illinois
b) Milwaukee, Wisconsin
c) Cleveland, Ohio

176. How many rooms are in the White House?
a) 500
b) 25
c) 132

177. On March 30, 1981, which one of the following attempted to assassinate President Ronald Reagan?
a) Dennis McCarthy
b) John Hinckley Jr.
c) Thomas Delahanty

Answers
173. c) Trump's senior staffers
174. a) true
175. b) Milwaukee, Wisconsin
176. c) 132
177. b) John Hinckley Jr.

178. When President John F. Kennedy was assassinated in 1963 the Vice President took his place. Who was he?
a) Lyndon B. Johnson
b) Henry Cabot Lodge Jr.
c) Dwight D. Eisenhower

179. (1963) After the assassination of President John F. Kennedy the FBI conducted over 25,000 interviews, followed thousands of leads, and found that the following individual acted alone in the assassination.
a) J.D. Tippit
b) Jack Ruby
c) Lee Harvey Oswald

180. (2024) Former President Donald Trump announced which of the following to be his vice-presidential running mate?
a) J. D. Vance
b) Nikki Haley
c) Doug Burgum

181. From 1963 to 1969 "Lady Bird" served as the First Lady of the United States and before that she was the second lady of the United States to which vice president?
a) Lyndon B. Johnson
b) John F. Kennedy
c) Dwight D. Eisenhower

Answers
178. a) Lyndon B. Johnson
179. c) Lee Harvey Oswald
180. a) J. D. Vance
181. a) Lyndon B. Johnson

182. Which president smoked 60 cigarettes a day then quit after he suffered a near-fatal heart attack in 1955?
a) Harry S. Truman
b) Lyndon B. Johnson
c) Donald Trump

183. When President George Washington took office in 1789 the President's salary was established at how much a year?
a) $10,000
b) $15,000
c) $25,000

184. In 1969 the United States president's yearly salary was $200,000. How much was it as of 2024?
a) $300,000
b) $400,000
c) $500,000

185. Who was President Donald Trump's vice president from 2017-2020?
a) Dick Cheney
b) Al Gore
c) Mike Pence

186. (1997) Which President issued an executive order banning smoking in federal buildings?
a) George W. Bush
b) Bill Clinton
c) Ronald Reagan

Answers
182. b) Lyndon B. Johnson
183. c) $25,000
184. b) $400,000
185. c) Mike Pence
186. b) Bill Clinton

187. To qualify to be a United States president how old do you have to be?
a) 21
b) 25
c) 35

188. The first President of the United States, George Washington, smoked marijuana.
a) true
b) false

189. If a President does not accept a paycheck, they have an obligation to donate it to an organization they choose. President Donald Trump donated his salary.
a) true
b) false

190. As of 2024 one United States president has resigned. Who was it?
a) Richard Nixon
b) Joe Biden
c) Hillary Clinton

191. On January 6, 2021, during the protest at the capitol, Ashli Babbitt was the only person who was killed that day.
a) true
b) false

Answers
187. c) 35
188. a) true
189. a) true
190. a) Richard Nixon
191. a) true

192. (2024) Secret Service Director Kimberly Cheatle appeared before congress to answer questions about the attempted assassination of former President Donald Trump. What decision was made the next day regarding her position?
a) she was fired
b) she resigned her position
c) she continued in her position

193. (2024) Who was the director of the FBI when republican presidential candidate Donald Trump was shot?
a) James Comer
b) Robert Mueller
c) Christopher Wray

194. (2024) At a congressional hearing, 20 days after the attempted assassination of Donald Trump, FBI director Christopher Wray said he had not yet determined if Trump had been hit with shrapnel or a bullet.
a) true
b) false

195. The Mount Rushmore National Memorial is also known as what?
a) The Badlands
b) The Prominent Four
c) Shrine of Democracy

Answers
192. b) she resigned her position
193. c) Christopher Wray
194. a) true
195. c) Shrine of Democracy

196. The land the Mount Rushmore National Memorial is built on was taken illegally from the Sioux Nation in the 1870's.
a) true
b) false

197. The 42nd president was the first democrat since Franklin D. Roosevelt to win a second term. Who was he?
a) Harry S. Truman
b) Bill Clinton
c) Lyndon B. Johnson

198. What is Kamala Harris's code name?
a) Joy
b) Sprint
c) Pioneer

199. What is vice president elect J. D. Vance's code name?
a) Smokey
b) Bobcat
c) Elegy

200. Hillary Clinton served as the Secretary of the United States before she became a First Lady.
a) true
b) false

Answers
196. a) true
197. b) Bill Clinton
198. c) Pioneer
199. b) Bobcat
200. a) true

201. All states follow the same requirements for someone to vote in an election.
a) true
b) false

202. Some states allow a person to pre-register to vote when they are 16 years of age.
a) true
b) false

203. (1974) When Richard Nixon resigned the office of the presidency his vice president took the oath as the new president. Who was it?
a) Dwight Eisenhower
b) Gerald Ford
c) Bill Clinton

204. Congressional records show President George Washington initially declined his $25,000 yearly salary but congress would not allow it.
a) true
b) false

205. What is the name of President Donald Trump's youngest son?
a) Donald Jr.
b) Chancellor
c) Barron

Answers
201. b) false
202. a) true
203. b) Gerald Ford
204. a) true
205. c) Barron

206. President George W. Bush's daughters, Jenna and Barbara, are twins.
a) true
b) false

207. What is President Bill Clinton's daughter's name?
a) Chelsea
b) Hillary
c) Heather

208. (2023) A video of two men having sex in a Senate hearing room was leaked to the media. The U.S. Capitol Police investigated and found no evidence of a crime.
a) true
b) false

209. (2019) Nearly half of all Americans still believe that which country interfered with President Donald Trump to win the 2016 presidential election?
a) China
b) Russia
c) Mexico

210. Since 1931 what song has been the official national anthem of the United States?
a) America the Beautiful
b) God Bless America
c) The Star-Spangled Banner

Answers
206. a) true
207. a) Chelsea
208. a) true
209. b) Russia
210. c) The Star-Spangled Banner

211. On May 9, 2016, which animal was named the national mammal of the United States?
a) American bison
b) Holstein cow
c) Rough collie

212. There is a Bald and Golden Eagle Protection Act that prohibits anyone from being in possession of an eagle's feather.
a) true
b) false

213. (2024) Where was the first presidential debate held between Donald Trump and Vice President Kamala Harris?
a) Des Moines, Iowa
b) Cleveland, Ohio
c) Philadelphia, Pennsylvania

214. President Richard Nixon is featured on a 32 cent U.S. postage stamp.
a) true
b) false

215. Abraham Lincoln is on the $10.00 bill.
a) true
b) false

Answers
211. a) American bison
212. a) true
213. c) Philadelphia, Pennsylvania
214. a) true
215. b) false

216. (2024) Who was the Iowa Governor that signed a law allowing authorities to take illegal immigrants into custody and return them to their countries of origin. Unfortunately, a judge temporarily blocked the law.
a) Matt Mead (R)
b) Kim Reynolds (R)
c) Laura Kelly (D)

217. (2024) The First Lady of the United States is referred to as Dr. Jill Biden. What kind of doctor is she?
a) general practitioner
b) Doctor of Education
c) pediatrician

218. (2024) What decision did President Biden post on X to his "fellow Democrats?"
a) to not accept the nomination to run for president
b) resign as President immediately
c) continue to run for another 4 years

219. The presidential car is a Cadillac. What is the car's nickname?
a) The Beast
b) The Caddy
c) The Panther

220. The governors in each of the 50 states earn the same yearly salary.
a) true
b) false

Answers
216. b) Kim Reynolds (R)
217. b) Doctor of Education
218. a) to not accept the nomination to run for president
219. a) The Beast
220. b) false

221. (2021) "The 75,000,000, great American Patriots who voted for me, AMERICA FIRST, and MAKE AMERICA GREAT AGAIN, will have a GIANT VOICE long into the future. They will not be disrespected or treated unfairly in any way, shape or form!!!" This was the first of 2 tweets President Trump posted on Twitter before what?
a) he gave a farewell speech
b) he moved out of the White House
c) he was suspended from using Twitter

222. "To all those who have asked. I will not be going to the inauguration on January 20th." This was the final tweet which resulted in Trump being suspended from Twitter because it was in violation of their "Glorification of Violence policy."
a) true
b) false

223. President Donald Trump joined Twitter in 2009. When the president was banned from Twitter in January 2021 how many followers did he have?
a) 1 million
b) over 88 million
c) 500

224. On July 1, 1847, the first 2 postage stamps were issued in the United States. How much were they?
a) 1 and 2 cents
b) 3 and 4 cents
c) 5 and 10 cents

Answers
221. c) he was suspended from using Twitter
222. a) true
223. b) over 88 million
224. c) 5 and 10 cents

225. (1847) The first 5 cent stamp featured the first Postmaster General. Who was it?
a) Abraham Lincoln
b) Benjamin Franklin
c) George Washington

226. The first 10 cent postage stamp was released on July 1, 1847. Which president was pictured on it?
a) George Washington
b) Thomas Jefferson
c) James Polk

227. (2024) More than 70% of adults oppose allowing biological males to compete on women's and girls' sports teams. Which president disagreed and said he would veto the bill if it passed the senate?
a) Donald Trump (R)
b) Barack Obama (D)
c) Joe Biden (D)

228. (1940) Who was the first African American featured on a U.S. postage stamp?
a) Martin Luther King Jr.
b) Roy Wilkins
c) Booker T. Washington

229. The highest Governor's salary is $250,000. Which state is it?
a) Illinois
b) Ohio
c) New York

Answers
225. b) Benjamin Franklin
226. a) George Washington
227. c) Joe Biden (D)
228. c) Booker T. Washington
229. c) New York

230. (2024) Which White House press secretary, under the Trump administration, is the governor of Arkansas?
a) Sarah Huckabee Sanders
b) Jen Psaki
c) Kayleigh McEnany

231. 2024) In what state did the governor's state budget proposal include $2.4 billion to house migrants without homes and help them apply for asylum or work.
a) Texas
b) New York
c) Florida

232. What is the capital of the United States?
a) Washington D.C.
b) New York
c) Miami

233. (2024) During the attempted assassination of President Donald Trump one attendee at the Butler rally was killed and 2 were critically wounded, yet critics of Trump believe he staged it.
a) true
b) false

234. Abraham Lincoln is pictured on the one-dollar bill.
a) true
b) false

Answers
230. a) Sarah Huckabee Sanders
231. b) New York
232. a) Washington D.C.
233. a) true
234. b) false

235. (2022) FBI agents shot and killed Craig DeLeeuw Robertson at his home in Provo, Utah while attempting to serve a warrant for Robertson threatening the life of which president?
a) George W. Bush
b) Barack Obama
c) Joe Biden

236. When a person recites the Pledge of Allegiance what are they pledging allegiance to?
a) God
b) the United States president
c) the United States flag

237. (2022) Which president set up a program, (CHNV) that allowed hundreds of thousands of migrants from Cuba, Haiti, Nicaragua, and Venezuela to fly into the U.S.?
a) Barack Obama
b) Donald Trump
c) Joe Biden

238. (2024) A program known as CHNV which allowed hundreds of thousands of migrants to fly into the United States was temporarily paused due to what?
a) President Joe Biden wanted to slow illegal immigration
b) DHS report found large amounts of fraud in sponsor applications
c) President Joe Biden wanted to end the program

Answers
235. c) Joe Biden
236. c) the United States flag
237. c) Joe Biden
238. b) DHS report found large amounts of fraud in sponsor applications

239. (2024) After the attempted assassination of President Donald Trump hundreds of thousands of tee-shirts flooded the market with what words?
a) Fight! Fight! Fight!
b) Don't Give Up!
c) Let's Fight!

240. (1975) Robert Philip Hanssen swore an oath to enforce the law and protect the nation as an FBI agent. In 2002 he was sentenced to life in prison for what?
a) murder
b) espionage
c) counterfeiting

241. When did the Biden administration announce they would end the public health emergency declarations that were brought on by the coronavirus?
a) May 11, 2021
b) May 11, 2022
c) May 11, 2023

242. The current design of the U.S. flag started as a history school project that was later submitted to congress.
a) true
b) false

243. A sanctuary jurisdiction can be a city, county, or entire state.
a) true
b) false

Answers
239. a) Fight! Fight! Fight!
240. b) espionage
241. c) May 11, 2023
242. a) true
243. a) true

244. The purpose of a sanctuary jurisdiction is what?
a) does not enforce immigration laws
b) does not tax its citizens
c) does not force citizens to license their pets

245. How many states are sanctuary states?
a) 48
b) 11
c) 3

246. Which state is not a sanctuary state?
a) Texas
b) Oregon
c) Washington

247. Bob Hefts design of the current U.S. flag was selected from 1,500 designs. Which president invited Hefts to a ceremony at the White House on July 4, 1960, to watch his 50-star flag be raised as the new official flag of the United States?
a) George Washington
b) Richard Nixon
c) Dwight Eisenhower

248. (2017) Which United States president ordered construction of a wall on the U.S. Mexico border to curb illegal immigration?
a) Donald trump
b) Bill Clinton
c) Barack Obama

Answers
244. a) does not enforce immigration laws
245. b) 11
246. a) Texas
247. c) Dwight Eisenhower
248. a) Donald Trump

249. (2021) President Joe Biden signed 17 executive orders in his first few hours as president. One order was to immediately halt construction of President Trump's border wall. How many miles of wall had been constructed?
a) 458
b) 50
c) 5,000

250. Who is the Commander in Chief of all armed forces in the United States?
a) the Secretary of Defense
b) the Secretary of State
c) the president

251. (2023) Dane county was the first county in the nation to become a sanctuary for transgender and nonbinary individuals. Which state is Dane county located in?
a) Florida
b) Minnesota
c) Wisconsin

252. What do the 50 stars on the United States flag represent?
a) 50 people in congress
b) 50 states
c) 50 United States presidents

Answers
249. a) 458
250. c) the President
251. c) Wisconsin
252. b) 50 states

253. Which president said? "The only existential threat to humanity is climate change."
a) George Washington
b) Barack Obama
c) Joe Biden

254. What is the United States Armed Forces' highest military award?
a) Medal of Honor
b) Nobel Peace Prize
c) Academy Award

255. (1950) What is known as the "Lavender Scare," was the investigation, interrogation and systematic removal of gay men and lesbians from the federal government. Which president implemented the order?
a) Jimmy Carter
b) Dwight D. Eisenhower
c) Donald Trump

256. (2018) Which president signed the Right to Try Act allowing terminally ill patients access to treatments that had not been approved by the Food and Drug Administration?
a) President Barack Obama
b) President Joe Biden
c) President Donald Trump

Answers
253. c) Joe Biden
254. a) Medal of honor
255. b) Dwight D. Eisenhower
256. c) President Donald Trump

257. Who is known as the Father of our Country?
a) Benjamin Franklin
b) George Washington
c) the current president

258. There are three branches of the United States government. Which one has the authority to declare war?
a) legislative
b) judicial
c) executive

259. You must be born in the United States to become a Senator.
a) true
b) false

260. (1845) When President Andrew Jackson passed away thousands of people came to pay their respects. What happened during the funeral that left mourners horrified?
a) the president's parrot started swearing loudly
b) the president's dog mauled a guest
c) the president's horse barged through the crowd

Answers
257. b) George Washington
258. a) legislative
259. b) false
260. a) the presidents parrot started swearing loudly

261. Several presidents enjoyed skinny dipping in their free time. Among them were Teddy Roosevelt and John F. Kennedy who had no qualms about doing which of the following while swimming in the nude?
a) singing loudly

b) playing music loudly

c) inviting others to join

262. (2017) The Trump administration announced that transgender individuals would no longer be able to serve in the United States military.
a) true

b) false

263. (2021) President Joe Biden signed an executive order to reverse the Trump administrations ban on transgenders ability to serve in the military.
a) true

b) false

264. Someone with a criminal past can serve in the House of Representatives.
a) true

b) false

265. To qualify to become a senator you must be 30 years of age.
a) true

b) false

Answers

261. c) inviting others to join

262. a) true

263. a) true

264. a) true

265. a) true

266. To qualify to be a senator, you don't have to reside in the state you represent.
a) true
b) false

267. There are no specific education requirements to become a senator.
a) true
b) false

268. (2024) While speaking in Michigan which president said? "You can't walk across the street to get a loaf of bread, you get shot, you get mugged, you get raped, you get whatever it may be. You've seen it, and I've seen it."
a) Bill Clinton
b) Joe Biden
c) Donald Trump

269. (2024) It had been a week since President Donald Trump was shot, and a congressional hearing was held to get answers. When being questioned, which representative accused the director of the Secret Service of being completely dishonest and said to her, "you're full of shit today?"
a) Marjorie Green (R)
b) Debbie Dingell (D)
c) Nancy Mace (R)

Answers
266. b) false
267. a) true
268. c) Donald Trump
269. c) Nancy Mace (R)

270. Steven Ford, son of President Gerald Ford, was an actor on what soap opera?
a) As the World Turns
b) Dallas
c) The Young and the Restless

271. (2020) As the honorary chairwoman of the Committee for the Preservation of the White House, which First Lady announced plans to restore and enhance the White House Rose Garden?
a) Hillary Clinton
b) Melania Trump
c) Michelle Obama

272. (2021) A petition circulated stating Mrs. Trump had "the cherry trees, a gift from Japan, removed from the Rose Garden." The media pointed out the trees were crabapple trees and replanted elsewhere. The petition signed by more than 43,000 people urged which First Lady to "Restore the Rose Garden?"
a) Michelle Obama
b) Melania Trump
c) Jill Biden

273. How many presidents have won the Nobel Peace Prize?
a) 6
b) 3
c) 4

Answers
270. c) The Young and The Restless
271. b) Melania Trump
272. c) Jill Biden
273. c) 4

274. Vogue Magazine has a history of featuring first ladies in its pages for the last 100 years. Over 50 president's wives have graced the pages. No doubt politically motivated, which First Lady was not featured?
a) Jill Biden
b) Melania Trump
c) Hillary Clinton

275. Which president established our national parks and millions of acres of national forests?
a) Woodrow Wilson
b) Theodore Roosevelt
c) Abraham Lincoln

276. President Franklin Roosevelt held office from 1933 to 1945 and lived in the White House for more than twelve years.
a) true
b) false

277. Which president signed the Civil Rights Act of 1964, which prohibits racial discrimination in voting, education, and other areas.
a) President Lyndon Johnson
b) President Thomas Jefferson
c) President George Washington

Answers
274. b) Melania Trump
275. b) Theodore Roosevelt
276. a) true
277. a) President Lyndon Johnson

278. When George Washington became the first United States president the capital city of the United States was New York.
a) true
b) false

279. How many different cities across the country have served as the nation's capital at one point or another, even if only for a day?
a) 1
b) 4
c) 9

280. (2024) To date there has never been a baby born in the white house.
a) true
b) false

281. President Grover Cleveland's wife gave birth to a baby girl in the white house.
a) true
b) false

282. When President John Adams first became president the Capital Building was in Philadelphia.
a) true
b) false

Answers
278. a) true
279. c) 9
280. b) false
281. a) true
282. a) true

283. (1908) Mt. Rainier National Park in Washington state was the first to charge an entrance fee to the park.
a) true
b) false

284. (2021) Which president signed an executive order setting the goal for electric vehicles to make up half of the new cars and trucks sold in the United States by 2030?
a) Richard Nixon
b) Lyndon Johnson
c) Joe Biden

285. (2019) Which representative from New York alluded to getting rid of "farting cows," in the so-called Green New Deal?
a) Alexandria Ocasio-Cortez (D)
b) Daniel Goldman (D)
c) Claudia Tenney (R)

286. September 11, 2002, the United States was under attack by 19 terrorists from the Islamist extreme group al Qaeda. Where was President George W. Bush?
a) mid-flight on Air force one

b) reading a book to school children

c) at the White House

Answers
283. a) true
284. c) Joe Biden
285. a) Alexandria Ocasio-Cortez (D)
286. b) reading a book to school children

287. What branch of government makes the laws of the land?

a) legislative

b) executive

c) judicial

288. (2024) A Planned Parenthood van was parked near the Democratic National Convention in Chicago offering free vasectomies and medicinal abortions.

a) true

b) false

289. (2011) Representative Gabby Giffords suffered a traumatic brain injury when she was shot in the head while speaking to constituents in the parking lot of a supermarket in which city?

a) Tucson, Arizona

b) Rockford, Illinois

c) Fort Atkinson, Wisconsin

290. The Quiet Skies Program was created as a response to the 9-11 attacks. It monitors passengers for potential security risks on domestic flights and airports.

a) true

b) false

Answers

287. a) legislative

288. a) true

289. a) Tucson, Arizona

290. a) true

291. Washington D.C. is a state.
a) true
b) false

292. (2024) Which representative for Hawaii said the following after being placed on the terrorist watch list? "It's no accident that I was placed on the Quiet Skies list the day after I did a prime-time interview warning the American people about how why Kamala Harris would be bad for our country if elected as President and Commander in Chief."
a) Julia Letlow
b) Tulsi Gabbard
c) Lisa McClain

293. (2020) Which president signed the Executive Order Protecting American Monuments, Memorials, and Statues and Combating Recent Criminal Violence?
a) Barack Obama
b) Joe Biden
c) Donald Trump

294. (2021) President Joe Biden signed an executive order revoking President Trump's Executive Order Protecting American Monuments, Memorials, and Statues and Combating Recent Criminal Violence.
a) true
b) false

Answers
291. b) false
292. b) Tulsi Gabbard
293. c) Donald Trump
294. a) true

295. (2024) Several states had attempted to keep which politician off the ballot? The states were stopped when the United States Supreme Court ruled that they could not kick the candidate off the ballot.
a) President Donald Trump
b) Kamala Harris
c) President Joe Biden

296. (1983) Martin Luther King Jr. Day was signed into law, although recognized by the federal government it took until 2000 before it became an official holiday. Which president signed it into law?
a) Barack Obama
b) Bill Clinton
c) Ronald Reagan

297. (2024) During a visit to the southern border in Arizona, which politician did not learn of an attempt made on their life until a newsperson asked him about it?
a) President Donald Trump
b) Governor Katie Hobbs
c) Senator Mark Kelly

298. (2024) A manhunt in Arizona turned up the suspect who allegedly planned to shoot President Donald Trump during his visit to a part of the southern border in Arizona. Who was the suspect?
a) Thomas Crooks
b) Ronald Lee Syvrud
c) Osama bin Laden

Answers
295. a) President Donald Trump
296. c) Ronald Reagan
297. a) President Donald Trump
298. b) Ronald Lee Syvrud

299. (2024) President Donald Trump partnered with country music star Lee Greenwood to promote and sell which item?
a) God Bless the U.S.A. bumper sticker
b) God Bless the U.S.A. t-shirt
c) God Bless the U.S.A. Bible

300. (2022) Which DA charged President Donald Trump with 34 counts of falsifying business records? Alleging Trump had his "fixer" pay hush money to cover up a supposed affair he had with adult film star, Stormy Daniels, a decade earlier.
a) Letitia James
b) Jack Smith
c) Alvin Bragg

301. (1980) The United States Supreme Court ruled that the taking of the Black Hills from the Sioux Nation of Indians required just compensation and awarded the tribe $102 million. What was the result?
a) the Sioux Nation refused the money and demanded the land be returned
b) the Sioux Nation thanked the government and took the money
c) the Sioux Nation demanded more money

Answers
299. c) God Bless the U.S.A. Bible
300. c) Alvin Bragg
301. a) the Sioux Nation refused the money and demanded the land be returned

302. There is a plaque displayed at the Mount Rushmore National Memorial that has which of the following written on it?
a) 1927-1941- Rushmore workers
b) names and birthdates of each of the 4 presidents
c) the Constitution

303. (2024) President Donald Trump owns over 2 billion in shares in his social media company and is 60% owner. Which symbol does the stock trade under?
a) TSM
b) DJT
c) MAGA

304. (2024) A few weeks before the Democratic National Convention President Joe Biden announced he was no longer going to run for president. How did he inform the world?
a) on live TV
b) a tweet
c) a letter

305. The president's plane is referred to as Air Force One. The vice president's plane is called Air Force Two.
a) true
b) false

Answers
302. a) 1927-1941- Rushmore workers
303. b) DJT
304. c) a letter
305. a) true

306. (1993) Which White House staffer filed a police report with the Washington D.C. police department alleging that Senator Joe Biden forced an unwanted sexual encounter on her? The case is still open.

a) Tara Reade

b) Deborah Ramirez

c) Christine Blasey Ford

307. (2023) Which advice columnist filed 2 defamation suits against President Donald Trump alleging he sexually assaulted her in the dressing room of a department store in 1996 nearly 30 years before she filed the suits. The columnist was awarded $88.3 million. It is under appeal.

a) Dear John

b) Ask Me

c) E. Jean Carroll

308. (2024) Which presidential candidate initially ran for the Democratic party nomination, but announced in October that they would run as an independent?

a) Joe Biden

b) Marianne Williamson

c) Robert F. Kennedy Jr.

Answers

306. a) Tara Reade

307. c) E. Jean Carrol

308. c) Robert F. Kennedy Jr.

309. (1938) Washington D.C commissioned a study to track the travels of what in Crater Lake?
a) a swimmer
b) a 30-foot log
c) a sockeye salmon

310. (2024) Who suspended their presidential race in August and endorsed President Donald Trump?
a) Robert F. Kennedy Jr.
b) Kamala Harris
c) Joe Biden

311. (2024) Nearly 6 weeks after the attempt on President Donald Trump's life 5 people were put on administrative leave. One was a member of Trump's personal protective team. And the four others were from which agency?
a) Butler Police
b) Secret Service
c) FBI

312. The United States Senate has how many members?
a) 50
b) 100
c) 2

Answers
309. b) a 30-foot log
310. a) Robert F. Kennedy Jr.
311. b) Secret Service
312. b) 100

313. During the 16 months that Democrat Robert F. Kennedy Jr. was in the run for president no network other than Fox asked him for an interview.
a) true

b) false

314. (2024) Alvin Bragg won his case, and a jury found President Donald Trump guilty of 34 counts of falsifying business records in his hush money trial. Sentencing will be after the November election. Although convicted of a felony Trump is still able to run for office.
a) true

b) false

315. As of 2024 who is the only First Lady to become a naturalized United States citizen?
a) Barbara Bush

b) Michelle Obama

c) Melania Trump

316. (2009) Four United States Presidents have received the Nobel Peace Prize. Name one.
a) Barack Obama

b) Bill Clinton

c) Donald Trump

Answers
313. a) true
314. a) true
315. c) Melania Trump
316. a) Barack Obama

317. President Barack Obama's two daughters, Malia and Sasha are twins?
a) true
b) false

318. (2007) Four presidents and one vice president have received the Nobel Peace Prize. Which vice president received the award?
a) Mike Pence
b) Al Gore
c) Joe Biden

319. (2024) President Donald Trump selected J.D. Vance to be his running mate. Vance is a senator in which state?
a) Missouri
b) Ohio
c) Alabama

320. (2024) Vice President Kamala Harris is running for president. Who did she choose as her running mate?
a) Josh Shapiro
b) Tim Walz
c) Mark Kelly

Answers
317. b) false
318. b) Al Gore
319. b) Ohio
320. b) Tim Walz

321. (2024) Laken Riley was murdered by an undocumented immigrant while out jogging. Congress passed The Laken Riley Act that would allow authorities to arrest undocumented immigrants who commit theft, burglary, larceny, or shoplifting offenses and would mandate they be removed from the United States. When Senator Ted Budd attempted to pass it through the senate the bill was blocked by which senator?
a) Sheldon Whitehouse (D)
b) Dick Durbin (D)
c) Susan Collins (R)

322. (2022) Three days after President Donald Trump announced his 2024 campaign which special counsel was appointed to oversee 2 pre-existing criminal investigations that alleged President Trump, and his allies tried to overturn the 2020 election?
a) Rudy Giuliani
b) Sydney Powell
c) Jack Smith

323. (2008) Who did President Barack Obama choose as his running mate?
a) Evan Bayh
b) Kathleen Sebelius
c) Joe Biden

Answers
321. b) Dick Durbin
322. c) Jack Smith
323. c) Joe Biden

324. (1992) Who did President Bill Clinton choose as his running mate?
a) Al Gore
b) Jay Rockefeller
c) Bob Graham

325. (2010) Which First Lady initiated the "Let's Move!" program with the intent to solve the childhood obesity epidemic?
a) Hillary Clinton
b) Michelle Obama
c) Jill Biden

326. (1997) Which First Lady regarded her greatest accomplishment as the First Lady was when she helped create the "Office on Violence Against Women?"
a) Nancy Reagan
b) Melania Trump
c) Hillary Clinton

327. (2018) Which First Lady started the "Be Best" program with 3 main focuses on children in mind; well-being, online safety and opioid use?
a) Melania Trump
b) Jill Biden
c) Laura Bush

Answers
324. a) Al Gore
325. b) Michelle Obama
326. c) Hillary Clinton
327. a) Melania Trump

328. You are required to destroy the American flag if it touches the ground.
a) true
b) false

329. (2023) A spy balloon was first spotted in Alaska and traveled across the United States for 7 days until being shot down off the coast of South Carolina. From what country did the balloon originate?
a) Russia
b) United States
c) China

330. (2024) A mysterious illness affected several people who were attending a rally at the Linda Ronstadt Music Hall in Tuscan, Arizona. Many people were left nearly blind. What is strange is that the only attendees who were affected were seated directly behind the speaker. Which politician was speaking at the rally?
a) Tim Walz (D)
b) Donald Trump (R)
c) Kamala Harris (D)

331. (2024) Mark Zuckerberg admitted that Facebook complied with the Biden administration's demands and censored relevant questions about lockdowns and vaccines during covid.
a) true
b) false

Answers
328. b) false
329. c) China
330. b) Donald Trump (R)
331. a) true

332. (2021) During covid lockdowns Governor Gretchen Whitmore went as far as to ban the purchase of seeds. What state does she govern?
a) New York
b) North Dakota
c) Michigan

333. (2021) During covid, although science did not back it, the CDC recommended maintaining which distance apart?
a) 6 feet
b) 2 feet
c) 20 feet

334. (2021) During the covid pandemic wearing masks was a requirement. When dining you could remove it long enough to take a bite of food or drink.
a) true
b) false

335. (2021) During the covid pandemic some private businesses such as restaurants and event promoters declined to serve customers if they did not present proof of vaccination.
a) true
b) false

Answers
332. c) Michigan
333. a) 6-feet
334. a) true
335. a) true

336. (2005) Condoleezza Rice became the first African American woman to become Secretary of State. Which president appointed her?
a) Barack Obama
b) Donald Trump
c) George W. Bush

337. (2021) The infamous "Fuck Joe Biden" chant began during which sporting event when a reporter incorrectly described the crowd as chanting "Let's Go Brandon?"
a) NHL
b) NASCAR
c) NFL

338. (2016) In protest of racial inequality, who was the first NFL player to show defiance by taking a knee rather than standing for the "Star Spangled Banner?"
a) OJ Simpson
b) Colin Kaepernick
c) Aaron Rodgers

339. The presidents live at the White House. Where do vice presidents live?
a) United States Naval Observatory
b) White House
c) their own residence

Answers
336. c) George W. Bush
337. b) NASCAR
338. b) Colin Kaepernick
339. a) United States Naval Observatory

340. Some politicians may have earned their unflattering nicknames whereas others...not so much. A few names that have stuck are, Pencil Neck, Turtle, Shifty Schiff, Tampon Tim, Comrade Kamala, Sleepy Joe, Jackass, Old Hickory, Tricky Dick, Old Granny, Sly Fox. Which of the following was called Orange Man?
a) Jimmy Carter
b) Bill Clinton
c) Donald Trump

341. Which state is nicknamed the Empire State?
a) New York
b) Alabama
c) Alaska

342. (1986) Clint Eastwood was not only an actor and director he also dabbled in politics and served as the Mayor of Carmel-by-the-Sea, California.
a) true
b) false

343. Presidents George Washington and Thomas Jefferson both grew hemp. Their concern was not how to smoke it, but what would be the best way to process it to make what?
a) candles
b) rope
c) shoes

Answers
340. c) Donald Trump
341. a) New York
342. a) true
343. b) rope

344. Arlington and Gettysburg are the only National Cemeteries in the United States.
a) true
b) false

345. (1999) Which professional wrestler became Minnesota's 38th governor?
a) Hulk Hogan
b) The Rock
c) Jesse Ventura

346. (1988) Which famous singer served as mayor in Palm Springs, California for 4 years and then went on to be elected to congress in 1994?
a) Sonny Bono
b) Prince
c) Elton John

347. (2003) Professional bodybuilder Arnold Schwarzenegger served as the 38th governor of California.
a) true
b) false

348.Which state is nicknamed the Aloha State?
a) Florida
b) Hawaii
c) Indiana

Answers
344. b) false
345. c) Jesse Ventura
346. a) Sonny Bono
347. a) true
348. b) Hawaii

349. (1985) Princess Diana made one of her most iconic appearances when she danced at a White House dinner with Hollywood star, John Travolta.
a) true
b) false

350. Benjamin Franklin was the president of Pennsylvania.
a) true
b) false

351. There are no presidents buried at Gettysburg National Cemetery.
a) true
b) false

352. (1971) Berkeley, California was the first city in the United States to become a sanctuary city, passing a resolution to protect United States Navy Soldiers who resisted the Vietnam War.
a) true
b) false

Answers
349. a) true
350. a) true
351. a) true
352. a) true

353. (2000) A purple state refers to a state where the vote fluctuates between the Democrat and Republican party.
a) true
b) false

354. Former President Trump is on the 3-dollar bill.
a) true
b) false

355. (2021) During the covid pandemic visitors needed a reservation to visit a National Park. After Covid most parks kept the rule in place.
a) true
b) false

356. (2021) During the covid pandemic most casinos closed. When Wisconsin casinos began to open, they took your temperature before you could enter.
a) true
b) false

357. You can join the Navy if you are over 30 years old.
a) true
b) false

Answers
353. a) true
354. b) false
355. a) true
356. a) true
357. b) false

358. (2021) During the pandemic auto repair shops were considered an essential business, therefore they were not eligible for unemployment compensation if they closed.
a) true
b) false

359. There are 4 states, Texas, Utah, North Carolina and Mississippi, that prohibit the sale of alcohol on Sundays.
a) true
b) false

360. In some states you can purchase alcohol at the age of 18.
a) true
b) false

361. (2024) In Wethersfield, Connecticut, when a state trooper was killed in the line of duty the town council refused to fly the "thin blue line" flag claiming it represented divisiveness and racism. They chose instead to fly the American and LGBTQ flag at half-staff.
a) true
b) false

Answers
358. a) true
359. a) true
360. b) false
361. a) true

362. (2024) Special Counsel Robert Hurs' investigation found that President Biden willfully retained classified materials when he left the office of the vice presidency in 2017. Despite the findings, why did he refuse to prosecute the president?
a) the president was not seeking another term
b) the president cooperated and returned the documents
c) the president was a well-meaning, elderly man with a poor memory

363. (2022) The FBI executed a search warrant on former President Donald Trump's Mar-a-Lago home as part of an investigation into his mishandling of White House classified documents. A year later he was arrested, booked and processed. The former president pleaded not guilty to how many charges?
a) 1
b) 10
c) 40

364. You can join the army if you are 40 years old.
a) true
b) false

Answers
362. c) the president was a well-meaning, elderly man with a poor memory
363. c) 40
364. b) false

365. 2024) According to the CRS if the Department of Justice decides to pursue a contempt case, violations can be punishable by a fine of up to $100,000 and imprisonment for not less than one month and not to exceed twelve months.
a) true
b) false

366. (1894) Which president made Labor Day a federal holiday?
a) George Washington
b) Grover Cleveland
c) Jimmy Carter

367. (2024) Which Attorney General was found in contempt of Congress for refusing to turn over audio recordings related to President Joe Biden's handling of classified documents.
a) Eric Holder (D)
b) Merrick Garland (D)
c) Bill Barr (R)

Answers
365. a) true
366. b) Grover Cleveland
367. b) Merrick Garland (D)

368. In United States history 3 Attorney Generals have been found in contempt of congress.
a) true
b) false

369. (2017) When a news headline read: "It's high time Barron Trump starts dressing like he's in the White House," First Lady Melania Trump thanked which former first daughter for standing up for her 11-year-old son?
a) Chelsea Clinton
b) Jenna Bush
c) Malia Obama

370. To join the military, you are required to be 18 years of age or 17 with parental consent.
a) true
b) false

371. Which state is nicknamed the Cowboy State?
a) Pennsylvania
b) Mississippi
c) Wyoming

372. Illegal immigrants make up 75% of arrests in Midtown Manhattan.
a) true
b) false

Answers
368. a) true
369. a) Chelsea Clinton
370. a) true
371. c) Wyoming
372. a) true

373.   (2023)   The   Oversight   Committee   began   an investigation into the Biden-Harris administration's radical open   border   policies.   Which   member   announced? "President Biden is the first president to ever unsecure a border on purpose."
a) Jim Jordan (R)
b) Jamie Raskin (D)
c) Jim Comer (R)

374. Who was the president of the United States in 2014?
a) Kamala Harris
b) Barack Obama
c) Donald Trump

375. Who was the president in 2019?
a) Joe Biden
b) Hillary Clinton
c) Donald Trump

376. Who was the president in 2023?
a) Joe Biden
b) Kamala Harris
c) Barack Obama

Answers
373. c) Jim Comer
374. b) Barack Obama
375. c) Donald Trump
376. a) Joe Biden

377. (1992) During the presidential debates George H.W. Bush tried six ways to Sunday to get out of debating Bill Clinton. In an effort to goad him into a debate, what did Bill Clinton's campaign do?

a) sent boxes of fried chicken to his campaign headquarters
b) sent 7-foot chicken mascots to his campaign events
c) tweeted on X how much of a chicken George was

378. (2022) Merrick Brian Garland, Attorney General of the United States, was impeached for endangering, compromising, and undermining the justice system of the United States by facilitating the persecution of President Joseph R. Biden, Jr.'s, political rival, Donald J. Trump, the 45th President of the United States.

a) true
b) false

379. (2024) It seems "Get Trump" has been the standard of the left since Donald Trump decided to run for office. Just when you think they couldn't squeeze any more blood out of a turnip, days before early voting was to begin, which Special Council issued a new indictment against President Trump?

a) Alvin Bragg
b) Fani Willis
c) Jack Smith

Answers
377. b) sent 7-foot chicken mascots to his campaign events
378. a) true
379. c) Jack Smith

380. Which state is nicknamed The Mount Rushmore State?
a) Illinois
b) South Dakota
c) Virginia

381. Which state's nickname is Ocean State?
a) Rhode Island
b) New Mexico
c) Colorado

382. (2024) Donald Trump did not know much about, nor did he participate in the framing of project 25, but the Harris campaign falsely promotes it as Trumps roadmap to unprecedented power.
a) true
b) false

383. (2023) During a hearing the director of the Office of Refugee Resettlement (ORR) was unable to answer questions about the whereabouts of more than 85,000 migrant children.
a) true
b) false

Answers
380. b) South Dakota
381. a) Rhode Island
382. a) true
383. a) true

384. Every state holds an annual state fair.
a) true
b) false

385. Alaska holds 4 state fairs a year.
a) true
b) false

386. (1984) Where was the last World Fair held in the United States?
a) Chicago
b) New Orleans
c) Milwaukee

387. (2024) Taking a ridiculous jab at his opponent J.D. Vance, who said? "My hillbilly cousins did not go to Yale, but I'll tell you what they did. They contributed to our community and they're proud of it."
a) Tim Walz (D)
b) Ron DeSantis (R)
c) Joe Biden (D)

388. The Hunter Biden laptop is Russian disinformation.
a) true
b) false

Answers
384. b) false
385. a) true
386. b) New Orleans
387. a) Tim Walz (D)
388. b) false

389. (2020) More than 50 United States intelligence agents signed a letter claiming the Hunter Biden laptop was Russian disinformation.
a) true
b) false

390. (2024) Which president dropped out of running for a second term after a poor debate performance?
a) Donald Trump
b) Joe Biden
c) Barack Obama

391. Which state is nicknamed the Lone Star State?
a) Texas
b) Ohio
c) Iowa

392. (2019) Who was the 17-year-old Covington Catholic High School student who sued several media outlets for falsely reporting that he blocked a Native American protester?
a) Joe Smith
b) Kyle Rittenhouse
c) Nicholas Sandmann

Answers
389. a) true
390. b) Joe Biden
391. a) Texas
392. c) Nicholas Sandmann

393. (2024) When referring to Trump supporters, Nancy Pelosi said, "they have become a cult to a thug."
a) true
b) false

394. (2011) A suspected Chinese intelligence operative Fang Fang, developed extensive ties with local and national politicians. Which politician was her most significant target?
a) Ro Khanna (D)
b) Eric Swalwell (D)
c) Terri Sewell (D

395. The Merchant Marines are a branch of the United States military.
a) true
b) false

396. (2011) Kamala Harris was the first woman, the first African American, and the first South Asian American to hold the office of Attorney General of California.
a) true
b) false

397. (2011) Former President Donald Trump donated to elect Kamala Harris when she ran for Attorney General.
a) true
b) false

Answers
393. a) true
394. b) Eric Swalwell (D)
395. b) false
396. a) true
397. a) true

398. 2024) A co-writer's family sued Donald Trump for playing which song at his rallies? Apparently, Trump supporters should not be subjected to hearing it?
a) Yellow Submarine
b) Hold on I'm Coming
c) Not Ready to Make Nice

399. Who was forced to apologize for saying this about Barack Obama? "I mean you got the first mainstream African American who is articulate and bright and clean and a nice-looking guy."
a) Joe Biden
b) Donald Trump
c) George W. Bush

400. (2024) During an oversight meeting chaos erupted when MTG said, "I think your fake eyelashes are messing up what you are reading." AOC said, "oh girl, oh baby girl, don't even play." Jasmine Crockett said, "I'm just curious, if someone on this committee then starts talking about somebody's bleach-blonde bad-built butch body, that would not be engaging in personalities, correct?" After the verbal exchange, who was asked to apologize?
a) (AOC) Alexandria Ocasio-Cortez (D)
b) (MTG) Marjorie Taylor Greene (R)
c) Jasmine Crockett (D)

Answers
398. b) Hold on I'm Coming
399. a) Joe Biden
400. b) (MTG) Marjorie Taylor Greene (R)

401. (2020) President Joe Biden said Donald Trump was "one of the most racist presidents we've had in modern history."
a) true
b) false

402. (2024) In an interview when Vice President Kamala Harris was asked if she had ever been to the border what was her response?
a) of course, several times
b) yes, I am charged with finding the root cause of the immigration crisis
c) I haven't been to Europe either

403. How many United States presidents owned slaves?
a) none
b) 40
c) 13

404. (2024) At the Democratic National Convention after delivering a speech, which politician walked over and shook his wife's hand?
a) Barack Obama
b) Joe Biden
c) Ted Walz

Answers
401. a) true
402. c) I haven't been to Europe either
403. c) 13
404. c) Ted Walz

405.(1992) Vice President Dan Quayle was long ridiculed for telling a boy at a spelling bee that he misspelled a word when the boy actually spelled it correctly. Which word was it?
a) potato
b) tomato
c) orange

406. (2021) His first week in office President Joe Biden attempted to move the country forward by issuing more than 3 dozen actions, all of them either reversed or ended President Donald Trump's executive actions.
a) true
b) false

407. (2019) President Donald Trump created the Space Force as a stand-alone sixth branch of the U.S. military and signed it into law.
a) true
b) false

408. (2023) A select subcommittee held a hearing on Investigating the origins of COVID-19. A former director of the U.S. Centers for Disease Control (CDC) testified how science indicates Covid-19 infections were likely the result of what?
a) pangolin
b) bat
c) accidental lab leak

Answers
405. a) potato
406. a) true
407. a) true
408. c) accidental lab leak

409. Tiffany Hennard describes herself as a "super mayor," but critics describe her as the "worst Mayor in America." Accused of many misdeeds, among her latest was to veto the board's request to launch a federal investigation into her alleged misuse of funds. Which town of 21,000 people is she the mayor of?
a) Chicago, Illinois
b) Peyton, Colorado
c) Dolton, Illinois

410. (2024) New Hampshire Governor Chris Sununu saved a man who was choking on which food at a Hampton Beach eating competition?
a) hot dog
b) lobster roll
c) apple pie

411. (2024) Under the Biden/Harris administration the United States Border Patrol has encountered over 8 million immigrants trying to cross our borders.
a) true
b) false

412. (1825) There were 2 United States presidents whose son also became the president. Who was the first president's son to become president?
a) George W. Bush
b) John Quincy Adams
c) John F. Kennedy

Answers
409. c) Dolton, Illinois
410. b) lobster roll
411. a) true
412. b) John Quincy Adams

413. When in office President Trump took actions that eased regulatory requirements, actions to withhold funding from cities that allow protests supporting Black Lives Matter, imposed stricter work requirements for federal welfare, prevent online censorship and promote federal civic architecture. President Biden revoked them all.
a) true
b) false

414. (2024) Referring to President Joe Biden who said? "He's such a consequential president of the United States, a Mount Rushmore kind of president. You have Roosevelt up there, and he's wonderful. I don't say take him down, but you can add Biden."
a) Jill Biden
b) Kamala Harris
c) Nancy Pelosi

415. Who was the special counsel that cleared President Donald Trump of the unfounded allegation that he colluded with Russia to win the 2016 presidential election?
a) Robert Mueller
b) Jack Smith
c) Robert Hur

Answers
413. a) true
414. c) Nancy Pelosi
415. a) Robert Mueller

416. (2024) When President Joe Biden was speaking to firefighters in Shanksville, Pennsylvania, on the anniversary of 9-11, a Trump supporter asked Biden to do what?
a) endorse Donald Trump
b) sign his Trump hat
c) try on his Trump hat

417. (2019) Three years after the election of President Trump, still unable to accept it, which former president said? "He lost the election, and he was put into office because the Russians interfered on his behalf."
a) Bill Clinton
b) Barack Obama
c) Jimmy Carter

418. (2016) Which presidential candidate said the following after she lost to Donald Trump? "You can run the best campaign, you can even become the nominee, and you can have the election stolen from you."
a) Hillary Clinton
b) Kamala Harris
c) Marianne Williamson

Answers
416. c) try on his Trump hat
417. c) Jimmy Carter
418. a) Hillary Clinton

419. In the early morning hours of September 12, 1994, while under the influence of drugs and alcohol, 38-year-old Frank Corder was killed when the stolen vehicle he was operating crashed into the White House. Which vehicle did he crash?
a) helicopter
b) Cessna 150
c) 1977 Pontiac Trans Am

420. What is Melania Trump's code name?
a) Gidget
b) Muse
c) Marvel

421. (2000) A blue state refers to a state where voters mostly vote for the Democratic Party. A red state the voters mostly vote for the Republican Party.
a) true
b) false

Answers
419. b) Cessna 150
420. b) Muse
421. a) true